# Relinquished

"A Heart Letting Go of Razor Strings to Redemption"

By

Rhonda N. Watts

© 2013 All Rights Reserved

# Dedication

This book is dedicated to my freedom and the healing from things that occurred in my past that encompasses the full spectrum of some of my life's experiences and even hopes as a woman, survivor, sister, and friend. I will not tell you this project has been easy because it has not but it is truly a major accomplishment in my life. There are many dimensions expressed that turns a piece of coal into a diamond over the years.

This book is also dedicated to some wonderful people that pressed the fact that God has something for me to say to help people. You know who you are and I thank you for speaking life over me and to me during this transition. I want to thank my children for them allowing me the space to write and encouraging me to be the best mother I can be. I pray this book will touch you and the lives of those that you come into contact with even if your faith is different from mine the effectiveness of life and its experiences transcends many barriers.

There will be more to come. Thank you for investing in my book and most of all thank you for allowing me to share myself with you.

# <u>*Enjoy the Read*</u>

*To the reader I am thankful to have you hold a dream come true for me. Please enjoy the poems and writings from the heart.*

*~Rhonda*

# Vision

*"All I know is that I am being written to be read for a mighty purpose in God" ~Rhonda*

God had a vision. He had a plan and in that place did His son stand for a sinner man. ME

His word came to pass. For in the beginning was the word and the word was with God, and the word was God. All things were made through him and without him nothing was made that was made. For you see the Lord knows the thoughts that He thinks toward me thoughts of peace and not of evil to give me a future and a hope. For God created man in His own image in the image of God He created him male and female He created them and blessed them (KJV). So on that note hello my name is whosoever believeth in Him shall not perish but have everlasting life. Ahhh, Life created as a masterpiece from the beginning. Perfectly formed and suited to meet the world. The world established as craftsmanship by God's precise instructions.

He said write the vision and make it plain on the tablets that he may run that read it. For the vision is yet for an appointed time but at the end it will speak, and it will not lie. Though it tarries, wait for it because it will surely come. It will not tarry.

So I stand as a vision to see vision behold vision "that's you". You are holding this book or reading this book as a manifestation of vision. To embrace gifts and talents truly glorifies God. So as I began to write it began to unfold that which is in my heart pulling on his will and not mine. For surely he gives me the desires of my heart. I write my joys, my pain, my victories, and my losses.

For in this writing some editing was needed to correct some typographical thoughts, deeds, actions of my own doing. God's grace covered them. He suited my instrument to perform well with His oil. Declared to give Him praise do I triumph over the enemy's plans to protect the vision that's coming to pass. Yes! Write to take the unseen and make it tangible. The unspoken captured written on paper from a tree where it ended but began when He died for us. You see I'm talking about vision. Gabriel spoke to Mary. What was to come became her vision to carry out and did she? Yes! Was it for an appointed time? Yes! At the end did it speak? Yes! Did it lie? No! Will it tarry? Yes but wait for it! So I wait.

I am being written (vision)! <u>I am being written for the ultimate purpose of God to stake my place in this world. Traveling the road less traveled to proclaim the goodness of the Lord and to reclaim souls back to the place where he knew us in our mother's womb.</u> SO here is the pen in the Master's hands writing on the tablet those promises of an expected end.

"I am being kept to be revealed at an appointed time for a mighty purpose for God"- **Rhonda N. Watts**

## Table of Contents

**ADORATION** .................................................................... 10
- A Room .......................................................................... 11
- Adoration ...................................................................... 12
- Alarm ............................................................................ 13
- For The Taking ............................................................. 14
- HE Breathed on Me…… ................................................ 15
- Rainbow ........................................................................ 16
- The Jewels on the Beach .............................................. 17
- The Masterpiece ........................................................... 18
- Watch Me ...................................................................... 19
- What Deliverance Feels Like ........................................ 20
- When God became my HERO ....................................... 21
- Who Am I? ..................................................................... 22
- Your Love Is Like ........................................................... 23

**DECLARATIONS** ............................................................. 24
- 12 Step Programs ......................................................... 25
- My Inner Me .................................................................. 26
- Recession ...................................................................... 27
- Righteous Indignation .................................................. 28
- Sssssssssssssh!!! ............................................................ 30
- The War Cry .................................................................. 32
- There's More To Me Than That ................................... 33

    Vision .................................................................................... 34

    YOU CAN'T HAUNT ME NO MORE!!! ............................................ 37

DIRECTION ................................................................................ 38

    Roadways ............................................................................. 39

    HAVE BEEN CALLED ................................................................ 40

EXPRESSION ............................................................................. 42

    All I Need You to Do Is ............................................................ 43

    Appraise ............................................................................... 44

    Crossing the Bridge to Can It Be ............................................... 45

    Daggers ................................................................................ 46

    Darkness of the Night ............................................................. 47

    More than Myself ................................................................... 48

    My Heart Cry for a Father ....................................................... 49

    Rampart ............................................................................... 51

    That's Cute ........................................................................... 52

TRANSPARENCY ........................................................................ 54

    Can't You See I'm in Labor ...................................................... 55

    Chamber ............................................................................... 56

    Expose the Bones .................................................................. 57

    I'm Just Saying ...................................................................... 60

    In Your Absence .................................................................... 61

    KEEPING SECRETS .................................................................. 62

    Message in a Bottle ............................................................... 64

    My Tears ............................................................................... 65

    Reverse the Curse ................................................................. 67

    The Phantom of the Secret Place ............................................ 68

To Be Mentally Raped ................................................................... 69
To Whom Much Is Given ................................................................ 70
Trust ................................................................................................ 72
Waiting ........................................................................................... 73
About the Author ........................................................................... 74
About The Cover ............................................................................ 75

# *ADORATION*

## A Room

I'm in a Room

Plenty of doors and special access granted

I'm in a Room

Scrolls of collected information

I'm in a Room

There are jars of oil

I'm in a room

Where the table top is shining like glass

Would you like to see more?

I paused and accepted the invitation.

I look down and I do not see my feet but a gown

I began to see amber grow all around me.

I see jade, amethyst, diamonds, and gold

I lose my breath...Suddenly I hear Come in here Beloved.

I try to fix my eyes on what is ahead of me but I am overtaken by authority and glory.

In this room I saw a room as I was in a mansion He prepared for me.

**Rhonda N. Watts**

## Adoration

He infused me

His love was infused on the cross

Infused into darkness for the greater good

of mankind.

The infusion while in the womb shows

naked exposure to a systematic flow.

I hear your voice Lord as you are

looking at what no man can,

the inside view.

The Lord says, I see and know all concerning you

My creation molded, shapen and made by My hands.

*Rhonda N. Watts*

## Alarm

Lord you are the air I breathe

I am living to live again

When you woke me this morning Oh lover of my soul

I was delighted within as I knew today that we would yet dance again

You are the reason for all I do

I never knew or had a love like this could be so true.

You have chased darkness from me and yielded me with immeasurable comfort.

I begin to tremble in reverential awe of you.

I am so embraced in your unselfish love toward me.

My lips form praise and my spirit leaps. I quicken inside that gives intimate tongues of conversation that flows into the atmosphere.

**Rhonda N. Watts**

# For The Taking

Gracious, Plenty, Fruitful are mere items on the shelves of supply. Virtue, Honor, Reverence are among them.

As I continue to look around I see worry, disappointment, strife, Buy one get two free. The bins are impressive and quite mysteriously empty. When I look around I could hear the conversations, Oh this happened and that happened to me. Lines of takers ......

I missed something but then as if the loud speaker came forth and a voice simply said, inside store bargain. When I looked down into my hand appeared a coupon with the word

"Redemption"

It is a done deal

~Rhonda N. Watts

## HE Breathed on Me......

Love breathed on me and I became.
Enthralled by the beauty that I have been given from within does my spirit sing....Praises from a place within my being where His breath resides. I honor Him with the fruit of my lips and the essence of my being moves to His delight because...I worship Him in spirit and in truth as it is my garment for which in Him I am shapeless but yet I move with the wind...His breath connected the unseen to the seen for the power that created me Was and IS...so I submit to you the passion that only can come from true reverence for the Master Creator of whom His breath is encapsulated in my vessel to bring Him due honor.
To my Creator...with love


Rhonda N. Watts

## Rainbow

God shows us the rainbow

A symbol of covenant

He shows us its shape through the clouds

We marvel at the handiwork of God. We look in fascination and yet we have seen many doors and many rainbows.

Today let your spirit soar high where you can see beyond the rainbow to the point where you are seeking the Creator of the rainbow.

WOW!!!!! In just that moment for a brief second, you did!

How quickly does the carnal mind rob us of that which is limitless for the limited?

Eyes have not seen nor ear heard neither has it entered into the heart of men the things which God has prepared for them that love him.

**Rhonda N. Watts**

## The Jewels on the Beach

Each grain is accounted for

so are your prayers. As I walk on the beach

I feel the sand in my toes; The Lord opened my eyes to behold intricate beauty. An array of colors and in them a richness and depth of which I can't articulate.

He began to tell me how these colors are vibrantly described in the Kingdom. I looked down in the sand and I found 3 shells. They were beautifully smoothed, colorful, and well-shaped. I began to treasure them in my mind. He said Listen just as one grain of sand is in its element, so are you. Just as you have found these shells are of my design so are you. In that moment I had a revelation.

One grain of sand can disturb a clam to produce a pearl. If I let a grain of sand be what it is, it can either be an irritancy factor or the tool to produce a jewel. A shell is to be left behind just as your spirit will leave your physical body. The jewel is what the Master has handpicked, which is me!.

~Rhonda N. Watts

## *The Masterpiece*

AWESOME WONDER, MAGNIFICIENT CREATOR Father, I thank you for your masterpieces. You have shaped each mountain by your design. You have set the dew over the mountains in the morning and kindled every creation to give sound from its earthen vessel. You know that as we stand up on this mountain we can release to you all the cares that we hold. We embrace your awesomeness. We want to come up higher. We want to release the weights that beset us from achieving our potential. Great things happen up on the mountain in your presence Lord. So we take this time to reverence the beauty that your hands have made. You set them for us to see something tangible outside of ourselves that you have done. You are limitless and our mind stretches in your leading and transfiguration of "Let this mind be in you which is also in Christ Jesus."

~Rhonda N. Watts

## Watch Me

As I flow...As I live...As I give

Watch Me

As I learn, As I GROW, as I flourish

Thinking on the things that once were. I hear you say...

Trust Me

My trust has been broken and now I hold on to the virtue of splendor bestowed on me by a King. For as I am in Him

I stand **ENRICHED** by saying

See ME

FEEL Me

Hear ME

Roar with passion within declaring the works of the righteous one to a land dry and thirsty for living water that bears fruit I say this to you

O taste and see that the Lord is good and His mercy endureth forever (KJV)

**~ Rhonda N. Watts**

## *What Deliverance Feels Like*

*Rain Falling*
*Music Playing*
*Songs being sung*
*Fresh Flowers*
*The dew in the morning*
*Raining my hands in worship*
*Bowing down in honor of God*
*Smiling*
*A Child's laughter*
*Fire Dancing*
*Dancing in freedom*
*A banner being raised*
*Cascades of joy*
*Freedom*
*Being Thankful*

**Rhonda N. Watts**

# When God became my HERO

Growing up as a child we are often influenced by the greatest commercials that list a hero for us. It may have been Barbie, Ken, Army Figures, Wrestlers, and Karate figures. Our eyes would light up when we saw these figures. We began to get excited for what we know them to be in our mind and we often try to imitate those things that have become indelibly imaged in our minds.

Coming up in the knowledge and admonition of the Lord, we have come to know that God is a jealous God. We have also learned that God is not to be mocked. The Creator was so great. He fashioned us so that he gets excited about us. On the best day of my life I can recall when God became my hero. I read the story about how God gave his only begotten son that whosoever believeth in him shall not perish but have everlasting life. EVERLASTING?!?!?! Wow, that means it will never end. No love of money or money can buy that. For He will never leave me nor forsake me. He will supply all my needs according to his riches in glory. It's a promise. So when I was a child, I spoke as a child, I understood as a child, I thought as a child but when I became an adult, I put away childish things. So I present to you my Hero, Jesus the Christ!!

~Rhonda N. Watts

# Who Am I?

**Colored by God**

Flavored by my ethnicities

**Clothed in Favor**

Fragranced by God

**Molded by God**

Saved by Grace

**Given a Name**

Adopted by Royalty

**Touched by Anointing**

Filled with Joy

**Righteously Received**

Victoriously Vindicated

**Worthy as a Warrior**

Kingdom Chosen

**God's Whisper**

Restored

**Healed**

Delivered

*I am who God says I am ~ Rhonda N. Watts*

## Your Love Is Like

The breath I breathe.....
Your love is like
The ever-flowing water in the sea, an endless promise with me
Your love is like the dew in the morning when I rise and tears come to my eyes
Your love is like a never ending fire. Lord you are the object of my desire
The air I breathe fills me. My eyes are made to see you and my ears long to hear your voice
Without you in my life there is no choice
Your love is like everything to me
Your love is like the night longing for you
Your love is like a song being sung in my heart
Your life is nothing I could ever live without
Your love is like a start with no end
Ohhh, Ohhh....Your love is like
The air I breathe fill me
My eyes are made to see you
My ears are made to hear you
Without you in life there is no choice...
That is what your love is like.
~Rhonda N. Watts

# *DECLARATIONS*

## 12 Step Programs

*Push through every obstacle*
*Stand to know you are a conqueror*
*Release your hold on the past*
*Capture the promises of God*
*Give of yourself time, talents, and substance*
*Receive every blessing from the Lord*
*Trust the true and living God*
*Bless the name of the Lord for He is great*
*Love, Conceive, Acknowledge, Accept and Deliver*
*Repent and return not to the former bondage*
*Know the power He has given you*
*Communication is essential so pray!*

**Rhonda N. Watts**

## My Inner Me

*Protected by an outer shell that is well put together seemingly strong beautiful and intact. Issuing words of comfort, protection, or encouragement just to name a few. Releasing prayers at the settling of the morning dew do I begin to dress in armor to suit me and yet out cries my inner me.*

*Recognizing that only my spirit is born again with much inheritance I do not forfeit my reign as royalty but this is a process of molding, shaping, building, and tearing down. Things that erected themselves in my life by form, fashion, or pretense, or experiences. You see my inner me is being prepared and is yet vulnerable, sensitive standing on every word. In the waiting do I face every form of being misunderstood, misused, and abused.*

*Breaking free to express myself only through the trail of tears that flag the viewer with encapsulated emotions. My mind wonders when the sweet release will come to bring about the shadowed case of this abyss into the marvelous light.*

*Arise and shine give God the glory for the story being written as "You" became the piece to speak to nations and speak forth that which you have sustained to bring glory to the Father. Clap your hands at the command to proclaim atmospheric change. My shofar sounds within as the anointing rises do I begin to release the revelation of reflection that what formed inside in now resonating on the outside. Hallelujah!!! The high praise to The One that took a piece of clay and shaped this as what I knew to be my inner me.*

~Rhonda N. Watts

## Recession

They says it's been a recession

It has been a lapse of time, a lapse of words, and a lapse of laughter

Sheer desensitization

They say it's been...

But I can only attest to the blatant reality of discord of pain, trials, and tribulations....Oh know this....

There is no rest for the weary!!

There is a realm of emotion that leaves by my body in the form of liquid extraction. There is pain. Ample supply, horrible screeching... and looting and violations to one's heart

So I come today on a blessed breath of that which has been given. I say, there is no recession but revitalization to a nation that is forgiven, healed and set free. Let these words serve as a declaration to a WORD spoken nation, I say

LIVE, PROSPER, & CONQUER

For these works are to be carried in the wind by the poet with a pen

~ Rhonda N. Watts

## *Righteous Indignation*

*Caught up in a perpetual haze of reality...*

*I find myself reflecting on the ecstasy of what was...*

*You see I lost myself, my identity to the unfulfilled promises of a golden sunset on the back of a white horse with sand cascading behind in its trail.....*

*I have the right to bring to your remembrance the days of once was*

*For you see in me is a righteous indignation that was birthed from a night of tears and a night of sweats detoxifying from your love...BUT YOU SEE.....*

*You gave me those assurances and you gave me that love that capped the doubt that would arise in my mind to the place of never-endings that seemed to find the place called shore.*

*Just when someone picked up the bottle to read me I faded in their hands because my identity was lost in their holding for not even my name was asked but my soul bore it's nakedness.....I have the right to revoke your license to read me do you hear me? Stop...Stop NOW....MY righteous indignation*

Was passed from your ear…to the lips, to the plank where your boys met the darkness, and invoked the experiences of privacy and intimacy of the heart to a place that was shot with dice to see who could compete for the grand prize…NOT ONLY were you playing the chance of life you also played yourself…

I have a right to voice my opinion for after all I am a part of you that has been removed by the smell of her perfume and the stride of her walk and the appraisal of her weight in matter of memory versus who I was …You kissed me goodbye…

You promised me….You'd loved me…You'd marry me….

You see I have a right to voice the injustice of the words not fulfilled by you and your illegal transfer to a different owner. You committed adultery and sold your soul for the "lust factor" not worth the equivalent of value you had in me…

~Rhonda N. Watts

## Ssssssssssssssh!!!

Hush now, don't tell my secrets

Hush now I say, your secrets are nullified

You see this is a war between my flesh and my spirit.

I am prepared to battle to the very end but this battle will not leave me wounded but victorious

For you see my secrets did not kill me for the resurrection has taken place

I release them from the bondage that once held me for my heart has had an excavation for evacuation

I release the weight of to a higher plain

### Sssssssssssssssh!

You see we are not blinded by our own circumstances but we are blinded by ignorance

We are not given a silver platter but given for pieces of silver. For on the trading board the enemy offers ransom

Your oasis is not refreshing but more a place of sludge filled water holes and quicksand to sink you deeper into an abyss

And yet you remain thirsty for my blood

### Sssssssssssssssh!

I say to you I am not a concubine to your insanity because retribution has been made on my behalf.

*I will not hold your lies as truth and I will not accept your image as beautiful, nor will I compromise for your fruit*

*Sssssssssssssssh!*

*My mind is no longer bombarded with the guilt you present because my mind has been washed*

*My eyes are not seared with images of pollution neither are my ears deafened to the sounds of your seduction.*

*I draw out my sword and I begin to say Greater is He who is in me than he who is in the world and I decree its stance on my life. For you see it's no secret that I am red, covered by the majestic blood of Jesus.*

*You can no longer speak to me to follow you for you are a stranger and I will not follow you enemy of my soul*

*Ssssssssssssssssssssssh, **I say***

***God is speaking***

*Rhonda N. Watts*

## The War Cry

The sound, the trembles in the atmosphere

The release, the anticipation, the raising up within

Ahhh, what is this sound that draws to the attention that very core of my being.

Overcoming, Victorious, it's coming...An Army

Some moving in stealth mode and others move more tangible. The sound, the sound, the sound out of the belly of those that feel the quickening... It's coming forth

All that has been in a time capsule for such a time as this we release the spirit of Esther, Elijah, and Ezekiel to go forth. We release the spirit of Deborah to go forth. The sound, the sound, the sound can be found in you.

Break forth through the spirit of fear and mount on the spirit of victory for this is your expected end.

**Rhonda N. Watts**

# There's More To Me Than That

*I wish you understood that there is more to me than that. I wish that you did not live in a fantasy and equate my validity based on who I was ...There is more to me than that*

*There is a time and a place for everything and you have kept me captive in your assumptions of what you think I want and what you think I need. You see that a change has taken place and it has to do with my future.*

*I'm not your door mat, your second hand mule; I am not the left over garbage from someone's table to be picked over. I am a real person with real feelings and real dreams.*

*It has been over twelve years of excuses and lies and more lies but you can see that there is more to me than that. You can't see the marvelous work in front of you any different from a T-bone steak and potatoes to put it bluntly. Oh how I am tired of riding in circles with you trying to find a resting camp. Don't try to bribe me, there's more to me than that.*

*You thought you had me; at one time you really did, but see that which is for a moment does not last, but that which is eternal does and the space you have tried to occupy is in violation to his arrival. The one...my husband to whom I pray for daily.*

*There is more to me than my inward quadrants and my melodic voice and the ease of my laughter. There is an intellect and a balance of wisdom that has risen up in me as a warrior. So I release you as an imposter. I am a creation that has found her rightful place in the care of the Master, The Shepherd, The King of Kings and The Lord of Lords.*

*~Rhonda N. Watts*

# Vision

"All I know is that I am being written to be read for a mighty purpose in God" ~Rhonda

God had a vision. He had a plan and in that place did His son stand for a sinner man. ME

His word came to pass. For in the beginning was the word and the word was with God, and the word was God. All things were made through him and without him nothing was made that was made. For you see the Lord knows the thoughts that He thinks toward me thoughts of peace and not of evil to give me a future and a hope. For God created man in His own image in the image of God He created him male and female He created them and blessed them (KJV). So on that note hello my name is whosoever believeth in Him shall not perish but have everlasting life. Ahhh, Life created as a masterpiece from the beginning. Perfectly formed and suited to meet the world. The world established as craftsmanship by God's precise instructions.

He said write the vision and make it plain on the tablets that he may run that read it. For the vision is yet for an appointed time but at the end it will speak, and it will not lie. Though it tarries, wait for it because it will surely come. It will not tarry.

So I stand as a vision to see vision behold vision "that's you". You are holding this book or reading this book as a manifestation of vision. To embrace gifts and talents truly glorifies God. So as I began to write it began to unfold that which is in my heart pulling on his will and not mine. For surely he gives me the desires of my heart. I write my joys, my pain, my victories, and my losses.

For in this writing some editing was needed to correct some typographical thoughts, deeds, actions of my own doing. God's grace covered them. He suited my instrument to perform well with His oil. Declared to give Him praise do I triumph over the enemy's plans to protect the vision that's coming to pass. Yes! Write to take the unseen and make it tangible.

The unspoken captured written on paper from a tree where it ended but began when He died for us. You see I'm talking about vision. Gabriel spoke to Mary. What was to come became her vision to carry out and did she? Yes! Was it for an appointed time? Yes! At the end did it speak? Yes! Did it lie? No! Will it tarry? Yes but wait for it! So I wait.

I am being written (vision)! <u>I am being written for the ultimate purpose of God to stake my place in this world. Traveling the road less traveled to proclaim the goodness of the Lord and to reclaim souls back to the place where he knew us in our mother's womb.</u>

SO here is the pen in the Master's hands writing on the tablet those promises of an expected end.

*"I am being kept to be revealed at an appointed time for a mighty purpose for God"*- **Rhonda N. Watts**

# *YOU CAN'T HAUNT ME NO MORE!!!*

*For years I knew you to be the boogie man. A man that was set to destroy me to devour me to take my soul...*

*You plagued my windows night after night and I saw you looking in on me...*

*Why do you haunt me? Why do you seek to feed on the terror of my innocence?*

*You sent out your hounds in my dreams to chase me down and run me until I had no breath...*

*You sent your aqua monsters to the pool and cascade themselves in waves and heaviness to drown my body...*

*You would send shades of dark phantoms to run across the room,*

*You would have those dark figures come out of the walls to smack me...Why did you do that to me?*

*I knew you were lurking around bringing fear to grip me...Guess what boogie man?*

*I grew up and I know who I am and whose I am...So now I won't ask you I will tell you because I have been given Salvation by The Messiah and no longer is my soul up for grabs...Know this ...You were created...but I was BORN AGAIN!!*

*You are the weakest link...Be gone to the dry places in Jesus name!!!*

*~ Rhonda N. Watts*

# *DIRECTION*

## *Roadways*

*I stand and I see you, perplexed by the motion of the wind.*
*My pain and frustration lead me,*
*Yet again to the split in the road.*
*Confusion on the trail to my destiny.*
*I behold my memory of purpose,*
*disguising my tears to blind my eyes,*
*from untactful direction.*
*Stepping out on the plain,*
*I drift out of control,*
*into a whirlwind of despair of who, what, when, where, and why.*
*Carry me to a place that is solid.*
*Instead of this sinking sand that immerses me.*
*In a dark, cold, and lonely place.*
*My cries for help are mistaken by the echoes of the tall trees.*
*That masquerade a picture called life.*
*Embrace me and dress me in vibrancy.*
*So that those that look upon me*
*can see what grace I picked up along the way.*
*As I yet stand at the crossroad called life.*

**Rhonda N Watts**

## HAVE BEEN CALLED

To be called is to be noticed

To be noticed is to be seen or heard

Only those that can see what has been given are those that are allowed

Only those that hear can go beyond what appears by sight, smell, and touch.

I have been called

I have been called to a place a secret place. A place like no other. A place just for me is called The Shadow of the Almighty

Now, I say that not selfishly because there is room for you. It is just that I have an assignment.

When I did not see myself worthy for this assignment, I began to remember the tears that I cried, the sleepless nights, the loneliness, the rejection, the hurts and so much more. I was being prepared.
I have been called

I am not a name that I do not deserve to be called, such as mistake, stupid, idiot, whore, and all profane things for I have a new name.

I have a newness. For you see I had been clothed with things of the world, and sold for a price. I wore garments that drew things like drinking, smoking, and sexing. Things that did not fit and were filthy. You see

I have a new garment now. A garment of praise, a garment of worship, a garment of intimate relationship to my Creator. You see I have been washed...

My breath is taken away from me as I try to get out the beauty within that can't be seen by carnal eyes or heard with assumptions

My body is an instrument of worship not a doormat for worldliness; I bow now in reverential awe to the Lord

My eyes are no longer dimmed but full of light and I pray show me your people the way **you** see them Lord

My hands are not contaminated any longer but filled with the fire of God for His purpose.

I have been called and I am blessed so I share with you a fragment of me and who I am now in Him

I sing a new song, I dance a new dance, I wear a new fragrance; I say Lord let your fragrance accompany me

In Him I am no defect but I am perfect because He said it is finished

I have been called

## ~Rhonda N. Watts

# *EXPRESSION*

## All I Need You to Do Is

Peel back for a moment and see the intent of my heart, to be free, to be loved, to be accepted..... But See

All you can fathom is your own vision, see how unconvinced your life is, and cause misery.

From the moment of conception there was a plan, yes even when you wanted to end it. God said no!! So here we are and I said and will say it again...

I release the pain; all I need you to do is...Hold Me God

A seed weathered by the storm

~ *Rhonda N. Watts*

## *Appraise*

My mind wonders at the thought of a true love.
<u>True Love</u> does it exist?
In the reality of the world of a woman that possesses jewels that are passed over as trash.
Items of no value, a worthless vessel on the outside.
While yet on the inside, she is set with the finest of satin & silk.
Her heart is to be one and her loyalty is priceless.
She has diamond encrusted eyes & emerald drops fall at her feet.
Her eyes are amber and her lips they are warm traced mocha lined caramel.
Her fragrance is that of sandalwood.
Her essence lingers to those that can capture her beauty.
These hands that hold me do you know my worth?
Do you know the true value you possess?
I see you looking at me.
Thinking of how you can fix me up & where you can place me.
I chuckle within as you appraise my worth.
Far below the Master's creation.

**Rhonda N. Watts**

## Crossing the Bridge to Can It Be

The ropes are old and worn from the element which left them badly bruised and beaten.

As I stand there contemplating on whether to trust my knower or dare not to cross away from my former life.

The bottles of uncertainty if I? Do I? Should I? Can it be?

I evaluate by my intellect and I could die right now if I fail or I could return to my former life and slow down the death process which is inevitable.

Ahh, what am I to do?

I have heard of those that have crossed over already and the great things and how they did not look back. I began to hear the voices that tell me don't do it. You won't make it.

You'll never be anything. You won't succeed. STOP!!! I remember the song how I got over. It becomes my reality. I seize it. Go for it.

All my promises are ahead of me if I just have faith, if I just trust in the Lord. I can do all things. Ok if this is my last statement know that I took the step.

I am now halfway across the bridge to Can it be. For I don't know how I got here but I heard the steps of a righteous man are ordered by the Lord.

**Rhonda N. Watts**

## Daggers

Daggers rip through my heart

Pain and sorrow does this vessel hold

Fear and Dread I do not welcome, for my home is of love & peace.

Through treacherous days and nights I fight to hold....

Yes....one more grain of hope to be delivered into this place called Rest...

I meet not death as a means of escape but only hope that this issue dies within me so that the new can flourish and a new day's dawn

~ Rhonda N. Watts

## Darkness of the Night

The sounds blaring at me…the whipping winds and clatter against my house

No place to take refuge so I think but yet I steal away to the lowest place for safety that is so far away

I lie down and feel the cold pressing against my skin cleaving to the most solid thing I know that is weighted but not tangible…I pray

Unleashing those barriers outside my quarters of protection are all of the ill planted memories and high speed chases that makes my heart palpitate

Hearing the sirens, the sirens, the siren and suddenly they begin to fade for I hear my heart beating louder than they

My fear grips me and my hands grow cold and my body begins to shiver and I managed to let one tear fall……………

To the ground it went and saturated the foundation on which I laid and I desired to be rescued but no one could hear me and I scream only to be silenced by the tornadic winds that are blowing away my menagerie of what I called life and………..

The darkness of the night surrounds me and I am left alone with my life flashing before my eyes from the least to the greatest of memories and in a moment ….I was swept away

*~ Rhonda N. Watts*

## More than Myself

I wish more for you than myself....

Salvation

True joy in the Lord

Health that does not waiver

Love that is limitless

Values, Morals, and Principles

Knowledge, Wisdom, and Understanding

Family- One that will not be broken

A husband to the woman who long to be loved

A wife to a man who desires one

Fathers to have and give respect

Mothers to nurture and establish identity

Anointing

Fresh and renewed relationship with God that your life would have balance

Prayer and Discernment

Financial Wisdom Applications

Restored Families

A Move of God in your cities ~ **Rhonda N. Watts**

## *My Heart Cry for a Father*

*Where do I begin? At the beginning? Or the End? Who, What, When, Where and What the Hell?*

Come on now we all have been battered and bruised by life in some measure but this that I speak of is a case to be heard by the highest Supreme Court...The Ultimate Judge

Conceived in a moment of passion and a feeling of release does he leave me. He leaves me to grow in a woman that is masked to keep me although her options are presented...Does he know me? I continue to grow securely in a place but I hear her cries for love every day because you were not there. She was young but she did not walk away...

The great day I came into this world was beautiful sunny and nice as I decided to come down the world grew cold and windy...SMACK!!! SMACK!!! Followed by the cries, you were not here.

I became that which I was seeking...and that was love fresh to the world and seeking security and that I did find but not in you. When presented because of my eyes and my skin was told I could not be yours...

You became someone's husband and my heavenly company became my brother who at present has returned to that state although I'm here...Where were you?

I have grown as a young girl thinking you were some remote hero only to find out the many disappointments and lies that have been sown. So sad...a curse of rejection passed onto me. For you knew not the love of your father and such became your life. A quest to love what was not loved moving from home to home, woman to woman, heart to heart.

I became your trophy and still in my teens tried to embrace you but no....You were gone for so many years how dare you step back in now? Your kindled anger pinned me off the floor and onto the wall in your dissatisfaction that I had a voice.

It was called Survival... and she was thriving within...I still cried for you...A validation is what I needed from you...instead avoidance.

Through conception more children came and then came my first child and living to see him die in my arms was more than I could bear...where were you? At the funeral did you show? Your support was welcomed but where did you go? On with life into my thirties I sought after you...

I moved you here and tried the life. I gave more than I received of everything only to send you packing... Why? You shamed me with your open rebuke of trying to be perfect when I only was doing the best I knew how again Survival...

I am heading into the stage of what would be forties and I release you as you are still making children at sixty.

Just want you to know God has validated me and He has never left me since the beginning. He gave you the chance but He fulfilled it. I cried out to God and He answered. I'm alright now. I'm free

~Rhonda N. Watts

## Rampart

My heart races as I run to find a hiding place...

I find no refuge in sight but that does not deter my plight....to live

There are the words that found me in my youth... "Take your time growing up"... "Enjoy being a child"... Yet my youth escapes this moment of where I am.... There is nowhere to turn... I breathe... The truth is...

This wall I keep running into is called my hindrance. It is my past, my rampart...my defensive wall that no one can seem to see but me...Suddenly...I hear a voice of someone unfamiliar yet comforting in the midst of my distress...

"I'm here, My Daughter, come unto me and I will give you rest. I will make all things new, no more worry, no more fear for I am here. I will never leave you nor forsake you."

I think to myself this can't possibly be with all that I have done and been through...To my amazement, I am swept up and embraced by His love and I see that the rampart, has been destroyed...So now I sit in this place and He has allowed me this grace and I hold the very peace that He has given me on this night...as my life has been blessed through an angel at The Helen Wright Center....

Rhonda N. Watts

## That's Cute

You know I have to chuckle within myself

and say that's cute...

You know I've never been one that has been one that gets stuck...

Feeling that I could be wrong and maybe I'm not but I say that's cute

I put my spin on what you call insanity and I say that is creative measures

And you say...You think that's cute???!

I say yes, it is cute because cuteness is not merely defined by physical attributes or contours of curves or nice texture of hair or perhaps even the finest of personalities.....

You know I have to stand back and regroup and defrag my mind from the placements of other's ideals on my life and say that is value when there has been no input from my Creator but rather from my competitor so I say...That's Cute

You say you know what I mean and that you have my back when in essence it is only selfish pursuit you seek and I say that's cute...

You create a word canvas of my abilities portrayed as Judas and I say that's is cute

*You strip my identity and pursue my place and issue my words as I would have given but even a thief knows a counterfeit and I say that's cute.*

*You want to play my role without life's experiences and when given over to the judges again I say that's cute....*

*Barreling down my journey of reflection and all that I could have done it does not compare to what I have achieved with marked credibility and when I realize this was never about contention or competition but merely recognizing that God the Creator of all of this had my days planned with an end...I say*

*That's Cute*

*~ Rhonda N. Watts*

# *<u>TRANSPARENCY</u>*

## Can't You See I'm in Labor

My contractions are getting closer and closer and closer

Five, four, three, two, one ....Breathe

With great intensity is this pressure bearing down in me. My heart beats fast, mind races, so much all at once I reach for you. Can't you see I'm in labor? Trying to deliver the seed that was planted

It was shaped in love or so I thought, But alas yours words come to me as venom. You speak only about your inconvenience but wait....... Wait! Wait! Here comes another....not much more of this can I take...Midwives on the scene, telling me to push...

I keep hearing you screaming at me as the dragon is ready to devour my baby......

Silence................................falls in the room as if it is sleep only to be awakened as Destiny is born.

~ Rhonda N. Watts

# Chamber

A heart yearning for a new start

Desperately praying on her knees...her silent tears expressing all her fears that seemed to feed from past hurts...

Yet forgiven

Recognizing he should not suffer does she try to buffer to tingling emotions yet being stirred... a soft kiss diffuses the blow of the sting of rejection....for on her lips a sincere seduction that brews from within with thoughts of passion being released.. He gazes into her eyes and receives life in a chamber he once thought had died...her arms receive him with loving embrace as she stares at her love face to face...face to face does she begin to allow her mind to race at the possibilities.... Of an answered prayer filling an empty space.

~Rhonda N. Watts

## *Expose the Bones*

*It is time to make room in the closet...getting rid of old things, old scars, old ways*

*Those things backed up, stacked up; those pictures, those cards, the pain that once were pleasure had become singed with unforgiveness and strife but again*

*I'm talking about a closet and the door is open allowing everything to tumble down before me it is as if my life is flashing before me but that which I see is dead...*

*On the tombstones of the memories says "Here lies"...but if we keep storing stuff in the closet I say we resurrect those things and cry out to God about the giants that slay me...*

*I take the bottle to my lips and those hands on my hips while my validation is coming through his tips of ... Unfulfilled promises of love and faithfulness but what do you know? This is my closet.*

*I take the razor to my wrists while I brace myself to meet his fists and then the smoke to tranquilize my lungs to face the reality of what I know to be but let me pierce my eyes to see but again this is my closet.*

*I take a look at a body once strong and firm and look at how my life changed when life was inside, the gift ...the gift of decisions and the decision to see myself as beautiful when equated with me being booty full of... you don't understand for you see the shelves in my closet...*

*Some are high and some are low nonetheless they are in my closet...Why you asking about my compartments? Yes, I have little boxes that fit in the big box that reads: Lies, Deceit, Truth, Rebellion, and there is ME*

Insecurity complexes vex me with years of comparison to the one that was my first role model and others to find my signature could not be written ....

I searched high and low to recall those memories that brought me great joy but somehow they have been smothered my poisonous concrete that has set with me for years in my closet. I have chiseled away parts of the edges to allow the water to seep in but yet blockages prevent me and hence the reason why my boots are lined with residue and they yes they are in my closet.

I'm screaming out loud and nobody can't hear oh yes this fear is trying to grip me. I'm banging on the door loudly and the storage space is expanding to the point of explosion but in a moment there is a sssssssssssssssssssssssssssssssssound a faint whisper. I look around and I find that everything around me seems smaller and a fresh wind begins to blow now I'm talking about a closet

I'm saying it is time to expose the bones that have been adding on since birth of things that were stored from my ancestors umm hmm those before me and those spiritual conditions that brought about tornadic activity and earthquakes that subdued me...yes chaos, being swept up and being consumed these would be generational curses that ended with the cross but I was shaped in iniquity and these things plagued me

*I'm keeping it real so that you can feel the magnitude of my expression I chose not to digress but rather confess because the devil can't have a hold on me and torment me in my mind because of the bones exposed. You may not understand but I pray you do. Again, I'm talking about a closet.*

*We need to be done with the things that contrarily please us and find our way to redemption through Jesus for with him He has opened a door that I can walk through*

**~Rhonda N. Watts**

## *I'm Just Saying*

Why tell you what I need if it gets more frustrating that you can't give it to me? I'm just sayin

Why tell me you care about me in words but your action is zilch! I'm just sayin

The words I love you translated into I lust you and your words become a strange tongue as you try to speak truth! I'm just sayin

Trippin over some ill wishes instead of laying down new dishes

I'm just sayin

Giving away what you shouldn't have when you realized it was the devil in disguise

I'm just sayin

Realizing your mountains are really molehills, change your lenses... I'm just sayin

At the end of the day it's still belonging to that day let tomorrow be what it is... I'm just sayin

*~Rhonda N. Watts*

## *In Your Absence*

I carried the tears, fears, doubts and dreams
I made sure that 365 days were covered
I found myself
I made sacrifices
I cried myself to sleep
I got a backbone
I discovered false love; I made false claims on love
I compromised then
I found God

**Rhonda N. Watts**

# KEEPING SECRETS

Hmmmm the touch the feel of cotton? Not....that is not the fabric of my life for you see

It begins with a story of a child who idolized her mother for her beauty and wit.

Who was faithful to her despite the guys who did not really love her Mom worth a dung pile...?

It was an appeal for action by generations untold called a curse....but it was a man

That actually made her "cherry" burst...

With great intensity did he penetrate her and telling her she was so sweet did he further

Delve into her pelvic chamber lifting her feet.

False claiming love was the desire he gave and to her it was the unmatched attention of a father.

She realizes this action would tear her Mother apart...This man...her daughter...her life. How much more could she sustain from a life of rejection and hurt? How many more pills and things to come to nullify the pain? Her concerns for her Mother....

Flooding with emotion of fears about being pregnant (in her ignorance of her youth) she looked into his unpromising eyes and trusted every word he said for did she know she was selling out her innocence in her mind to be loved only to truly be raped...

The silence....The argument of why did she feel this way? How did he touch me to seduce me into sowing into me those spirits of his lusts...?

Confusion, Cloudiness of mind why not cry for help?

Who would believe?

Something is happening....My mind goes black and I feel so withdrawn but the naturalness of my body is taking in the very thing that I used to hear in the bedroom next door with pain and ease to not tear me

Shhhhh....Shhhhhhh this would be our secret between me and you.... You can't tell nobody while he made me feel to be so important and special for what He felt he gave me. I was manipulated into feeling it was ok and not knowing this action caused me to see different the rest of my life...Keeping secrets... now that the story has been told.. It seems that I would be dead because surely this man gave more than his share and all these years I would hold a secret from my mother that I would not dare. I figured God would get him for what he did to me and spare the life of humanity for God's punishment would be far greater than that of My Mother........Keeping Secrets...I was asked about it and I denied it. I protected him. I protected my mother but I left myself vulnerable to the devil all these years. Keeping secrets? I release you so that I can live free because I found Jesus and He came to set the captives free....

~Rhonda N. Watts

## Message in a Bottle

*Your words quench my thirst, when I think of you*

Miles separate us but love unites us heart to heart and your smile brightens the darkest of nights. I begin to think and my mind takes flight to a place of pleasurable emotions that settles the commotion of my oneness I long for you to hold me. A place of security where I am free. Your strength feeds my weakness in your eyes is the receipt of acceptance from every form of pretense... Your licked lips make love to mine and remind me of times past when we were together before miles separated us. My thoughts are as texts released into an atmosphere that I pray lands on a tender heart. Your breath on my body blankets me from the cold of which my breath pauses until the release....the walks, the sand, the water I yearn and does the passion for you burn like when you smile, giggle, and moan. Yes even when you moan

Those things even when you look so lovingly into my eyes and the serenade they sing to me I melt more and more into you. They say beware of wolves in sheep's clothing but what about this? A wild side topped with gentleness not literally but figuratively... I keep watch in my prayers

I bless, I cover, and I love therefore Love is made sweet... For this message could be delivered by a dove, but for you my love this message is in a bottle sealed until you open me, once more, and again, and again... My Husband is anticipating me as I am anticipating him...

~Rhonda N. Watts

# My Tears

My tears were clear but now they are colored for the many storms that I have gone through in this life

My tears have healed, my tears have held laughter, and my tears have shown pain

My Tears

Are a weapon of release from the things of which my eyes and what my heart can't fathom

My Tears

Have offered up repentance for generations past, present, and future and they have been cloudy with deep compassion

My Tears

Have flowed down my face at the birth of my children and at their transition way too early in life did they go and my tears are now kept for them by God

My Tears

For those that remain are of the deepest love that one could feel and yet they will be there as a reminder of the joys that compensates for temporary absence.

My Tears

Are not to be confused as a sign of weakness for in them lies great strength and weight of endurance...I say great is the Lord and all His ways...

My Tears

Are kept by God and in that they are safe for He knows the story that each one held and He knows the story for tomorrow but for now at least this very moment.....

My Tears are kept by God

**~ Rhonda N. Watts**

## *Reverse the Curse*

*Reverse the curse that has followed me...*
*Reverse the curse that has a name of promiscuity...*
*Reverse the curse of malignant poison in your veins...*
*Reverse the curse of broken covenants...*
*Reverse the curse of love validated on your back...*
*Reverse the curse of pharmaceutical seduction...*
*Reverse the curse of liquid intoxication...*
*Reverse the curse of regret which you shall not forget...*
*Reverse the curse of mental stagnation of depression, oppression and manipulation...*
*Reverse the curse I say!*
*Reverse the curse of dissatisfaction of your skin and skills...*
*Reverse the curse to start over and never go back AGAIN!*

**Rhonda N. Watts**

## The Phantom of the Secret Place

You take center stage.
The lights, the camera, and my eyes are fixated on you.
Your voice behind my ears numbs me from rational thoughts.
Your touch penetrates me.
I want to run.
I am completely tranquilized in your passion.
The heat of your breathe on my neck feels like fire.
I jerk and you comfort me in your embrace.
I feel like I can let go with you.
I feel like I am in a whirlwind.
I feel so…
Your mask: will you reveal your heart to me?
Suddenly, you vanish at dawn.
Why have you come in only to run out?
Why have you ignited this within me and run away?
What is it? Tell me.
Please come back.
I long for your presence.
More and more of you I am waiting.

**Rhonda N. Watts**

## To Be Mentally Raped

You hear tragedy, victim, injustice, hurt, pain, anguish, frustration just to name a few

I have been mentally raped.

Raped, by stripping my mind to images and scenes on television that had become known as reality.

Random acts of violence, senselessness,

Mentally raped to the visions of death of military tragedy.

Child molestation, sexual indecisiveness, false images, false hopes.

I have been mentally raped by those that walked with me casting all their cares not even asking about me.

I have been mentally raped. Torn down by who I thought myself to be. Only to be reimaged by someone else's expectation.

I have been mentally raped by lovers that made promises and left them empty.

I have been mentally raped by losing my identity in the things I desired to performing ritualistic duties of the decisions made by my life. I have been....

The essence of who I am and who I desire to be is not fully encompassed with a new ray of hope filled with an insatiable desire to succeed past my pain. I stumbled on these words...

Let this mind be in you which is also in Christ Jesus (KJV).

**Rhonda N. Watts**

## *To Whom Much Is Given*

Given…to whom? I did not ask for this so how did it become required. Tell me was it unclaimed dreams? Unmentionable disappointments? Was it those experiences of living others dreams through my own? Oh wait! Was it the fatherless nation that I have come to stake my place as a seed of its harvest?

Don't cast your pearls? Wait! Isn't that a requirement or maybe it was a lie to have me give more of myself than I could afford…

When Martin L. King said he had a dream oh what liberation and freedom spoken over closed gates that heard the sound of a melody released from Heaven.

Given the man/woman on the streets due to abandonment, drugs, abuse, finance collapse, family, or whatever. Given

A child born with no arms yet can write, sing, dance, and give of that which was unconditional to conditional mindsets…

Given

Given- standing for righteousness as one counted unrighteousness until the blood was shed paying the costs
GIVEN MUCH REQUIRED

Me to assess the very integral part of me that has chosen to open up the port and allow the rivers of emotion and passion about life and all of its idiosyncrasies. COME NOW!!

*I tell you my much has been given in patience for while I scream loud there is no sound while I beat my fist upon my knee you see injustice. WAKE UP oh sleepers someone is keeping an eye on you don't you know it? They are called dream catchers tangling webs to weave that which is sacred. GIVEN is being that support to others dreams who are awake and being a part of a team only to realize you've been cut! GIVEN to sow seeds in prayer and carrying out the best of intentions to others, but you were broken when used up and over no more use. GIVEN!!*

*Cry loud spare not who hears you? The pillows, your palms, that shoulder? GIVEN*

*It isn't what it used to be. What happened that you gave your all and got nothing in return? GIVEN*

*To whom you may ask? Well if we are honest it simply is you, you and you!!! Take a good look in the mirror*

See your given, that which you gave. Is it commensurate to the ultimate price given? No it's not merely chump change on the dollar much less a block of gold. Don't neglect the writing of that which needs to be told... Be Bold, Be Free, Be Intentional

It was never a second thought when what became required surrendered to the process. That to whom became Him who allows me to be given.

**~Rhonda N. Watts**

## Trust

A life without trust can make you vulnerable to the elements of life......If life were not already sustained in the breath I breathe I could at least attest to the fact that I or rather my body has trusted but my heart so desperately is seeking to be resuscitated beyond the hurt of daggers of distrust or eyes that cut me where I would bleed within. Tell me trust is given as it is earned but behind closed doors do you reach for me only to squeeze out one last drop. Oh how I am seared in my skin for the discontentment arises...

Why am I here?

What is this?

When Will I come to know it?

To be sweetened with flattery of words from a bitter tongue I shew you for love not comes from you!! My ears are hot from accusations and my tear ducts bleed sand...My voice is silenced for the lump swelling in my throat.

Can you tell me how to trust? Can you tell me how I can get it?

My first impulse was to run but God had me to sit still... I trust that this is right. Did I just say that? It was not me. It is my spirit making a declaration in what does seem to be in this realm. When the umbilical cord was cut trust was established and as arms held me trust was standing beside me to break my fall....I'm crying, pleading, my Lord please break down the walls ...

Signed,

A wounded Soul Rhonda N. Watts

# Waiting

"It's worth it. Wait for it."

That's what I've been told but can I just be real for a minute?

Waiting is painful, frustrating, and lonely not to mention depressing at times. Waiting can mean too much time on your hands too much to get into...

What mess can be created from unbearable impatience? Waiting for you, for it, or that special someone let me not just have a fit but rather spit the release of this present imprisonment called waiting.

I'm angry, I'm mad, I'm confused looking around for the answer to pop out the wall, the ceiling, the floor SOMETHING!!

I grit my teeth not from jealousy of others occupying space that was created for me yet I am freaking waiting. C'mon God!! Can't you see me I'm doing it. Okay yes having a brat fit but see no one ever said waiting was easy but I am here, right here, tears, sweat, and snot with time on my hands yet I'm waiting, waiting, waiting!

~Rhonda N. Watts

## About the Author

Rhonda Watts is a native of Lexington, Virginia. She is the mother of two children, Jaron and Naijah, and currently resides in Raleigh, North Carolina. Rhonda is very passionate about people and her love for people allows her to fulfill her purpose in ministry. Rhonda has also developed a characters known as Glendora LeChic Jenkins & Aunt Beulah Jenkins who utilizes Christian comedy. Rhonda has written plays to help people understand the importance of healing and deliverance through laughter.

To find out more about Glendora LeChic Jenkins please visit Facebook or email her at glendoralechicjenkins@hotmail.com

Follow Me on Twitter @RhondaNic

Follow Glendora on Twitter @GlendoraLeChicJ

## About The Cover

The cover of this book was designed and painted by Shawn Etheridge of Shawn Etheridge Art. This piece is chosen from his Every Day Angels collection. Shawn has been an artist for over 30 years in which has been painting, drawing, sculpting, singing, and music production. He and his family reside in Raleigh, NC. He is happily married to Shanika Etheridge and they have three beautiful children in which he gives God all the glory for truly without him none of his accomplishments would be possible.

For more information about Shawn Etheridge

www.facebook.com/S.E.Originals.Art

www.illastrasshawn@gmail.com

Or

Contact Shawn at 919-819-1697

www.ingramcontent.com/pod-product-compliance
Lightning Source LLC
Chambersburg PA
CBHW072014060426
42446CB00043B/2482